Remembering
Chicago
Crime in the Capone Era

John Russick

T U R N E R
PUBLISHING COMPANY

Police detectives reenact the St. Valentine's Day Massacre in the garage at 2122 N. Clark where the murders took place. The killers lined up six gangsters and one other man and opened fire with machine guns that had been concealed under their coats.

Remembering Chicago

Crime in the Capone Era

Turner Publishing Company
www.turnerpublishing.com

Remembering Chicago: Crime in the Capone Era

Library of Congress Control Number: 2010924307

ISBN: 978-1-59652-651-8

Printed in the United States of America

ISBN 978-1-68336-816-8 (pbk.)

CONTENTS

Captain Joseph Goldberg examines contraband beer and booze found in a raid. Prohibition and the subsequent illegal trade in alcohol was a catalyst for the gang wars during Capone's time.

ACKNOWLEDGMENTS

This book would not be possible without the assistance of two talented researchers, Cortney K. Tunis and Isabella J. Horning. They worked under extremely tight deadlines to review original source materials and investigate image dates, places, and names.

I want to thank the Chicago History Museum staff members who helped reproduce all the images for this volume, specifically Debbie Vaughan, Director of Research and Access and Chief Librarian; Rob Medina, Rights and Reproductions Coordinator; Bryan McDaniel and Erin Tikovitsch, Rights and Reproductions Assistants; John Alderson, Senior Photographer; and Jay Crawford, Photographer.

Last, I want to thank Gary T. Johnson, President, and Russell Lewis, Executive Vice President and Chief Historian, of the Chicago History Museum for giving me the opportunity to write the text for this book.

_____

For Susan, Leo, and Sofia

Introduction
Chicago in the Capone Era

It is quite a challenge to caption photographs about the Chicago underworld in the 1920s, a place inhabited by characters who wished to remain anonymous, who concealed their true identities and masqueraded as simple businessmen or even defenders of the poor, and who conducted their illicit trade behind closed doors to protect both themselves and their customers.

Pictures of cloaked figures in trench coats and fedoras, and policemen raiding speakeasies, breaking up beer barrels, and smashing stills, tend only to reflect how the gangs behaved when they were out of the shadows, and how the policemen looked when they were aware of the presence of cameras. A collection of these images alone might fail to reveal anything but the theater the public was meant to see.

Chicago in the Roaring Twenties was more than just a violent playground for the gangs. The U.S. census in 1920 revealed that for the first time in American history more people lived in the nation's cities than in rural areas. Cities like Chicago experienced a tremendous influx of people from across America searching for a better life. Laborers, musicians, social activists—and gangsters—all came. They brought with them energy, ambition, and determination to "make it" in Chicago.

Perhaps no other decade in American history conjures more romantic notions than the 1920s. Too often the realities of the corruption, greed, gang violence, racial prejudice, and gender inequality that shaped the decade are lost in the seductive image of the flapper, the allure of speakeasies and forbidden nightclubs, or the brilliance of an original Louis Armstrong solo. It must be remembered that the flamboyant and independent flapper emerges after more than a half-century-long struggle for equality by American women. Speakeasies were run by ruthless gangsters and hoodlums who dared defy the Volstead Act and defended their turf in violent gun battles. And Louis Armstrong is a symbol of the great flood of African Americans who left the South in search of a better life and freedom of expression in the nation's northern cities.

This book tries to paint a rich portrait of Chicago when gangsters, such as George "Bugs" Moran, John Torrio, Dean O'Banion, Earl "Hymie" Weiss, and "Scarface" Al Capone, operated multi-million-dollar illegal operations, used intimidation, extortion, and bribery to get their way, and regularly killed one another to satisfy their greed or their egos. It is hoped that this collection of photographs will provide some clarity and insight into Chicago's complex relationship with the gangs of the Capone era.

—John Russick

Facing south toward north Michigan Avenue. The scene is dominated by the Palmolive building, an Art Deco masterpiece designed by Holabird and Root and completed in 1929. At the top of the building stood the Lindbergh beacon, named for Charles Lindbergh, the American aviator who flew solo across the Atlantic Ocean in 1927 and became an international celebrity.

Chicago in the Roaring Twenties

(1900–1920s)

On Armistice Day large crowds marched down Michigan Avenue in celebration of peace. Here, crowds gather in front of the Art Institute of Chicago.

A pro-suffrage gathering in downtown Chicago at the corner of Van Buren Street and Michigan Avenue, June 16, 1916. The women's suffrage movement lasted from roughly the 1860s to 1920. Many progressive women involved in the movement for suffrage also championed the abolition of alcohol.

The original Juvenile Court Building and Detention Home near the corner of Halsted and Des Plaines streets. Chicago was the first city in the United States to establish a separate court to cater to the specific needs of juvenile offenders.

This saloon was located at 4183 S. Halsted Street. Prior to prohibition, saloons served as community centers, especially in areas of the city where literacy rates were low, and where social drinking was common and widely accepted. In Chicago, German and Irish immigrants converted saloons into cultural enclaves. Breweries controlled saloons and rented to barkeeps. As the price of licenses increased due to the growing influence of the temperance movement, saloonkeepers began to rely on gangs to support their businesses.

Police officers with distilling equipment. The U.S. Commissioner of Prohibition reported that, in the twelve months between July 1929 and June 1930, agents seized more than 16,000 distilleries and more than 8,000 stills, nationwide.

During the race riot, Chicago's mostly white police force proved to be ineffectual, and only the state militia and a subduing rainfall quelled the violence.

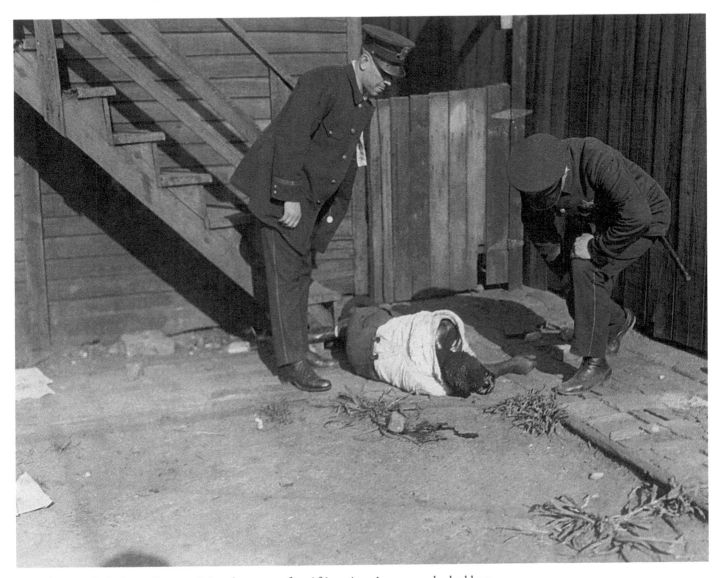

This photograph depicts police examining the corpse of an African American man who had been stoned and beaten to death. The riots resulted in the deaths of 15 whites and 23 blacks and an additional 537 people injured. The riot ended, but Chicago's race equation changed little, if it all.

Shown here, White Sox players Chick Gandil, Eddie Cicotte, Charles "Swede" Risberg, Fred McMullin, Claude "Lefty" Williams, George "Buck" Weaver, "Shoeless" Joe Jackson, and Oscar "Happy" Felsch were charged with conspiracy to defraud the public, to commit a confidence game, and to injure the business of owner Charles A. Comiskey. The trial lasted 14 days, and on August 2, 1921, the players were found not guilty, despite the fact that many of them had confessed to knowing of, or participating in, the scheme.

Despite their acquittal, the first-ever baseball commissioner Kenesaw Mountain Landis, seated and surrounded by baseball franchise owners, expelled all eight players from Major League Baseball to reassure the public as to the purity of America's beloved pastime. The Black Sox scandal contributed to Chicago's reputation for corruption and vice.

At the dawn of the 1920s, few people had ever flown in an airplane. In the few years between the Wright brothers' first flights and the emergence of the image of the dashing World War I flying ace, flight had captured the imagination of America. After the war, air shows, barnstorming acts, and wing-walking became wildly popular, and Charles Lindbergh's nonstop, solo flight across the Atlantic in 1927 symbolized the freedom, technological advances, and the possibilities of the era.

Chicago, like most of America, prospered in the 1920s. The city, and its reputation, grew dramatically. The Drake Hotel, owned by brothers Tracy and John Drake and designed by architects Marshall and Fox, opened on New Years Day 1920 and hosted Chicago's elite throughout the 1920s.

Founded in 1893 by one of Chicago's richest men, Marshall Field, the Field Museum's first incarnation was part of the World's Columbian Exposition Palace of Fine Arts in Jackson Park. After the fair, plans were drawn up to move the Field collection to its current home in Grant Park. World War I delayed the opening of the Field Museum, shown here, and the building was converted to a hospital for soldiers. Eventually construction of the museum was completed, and on May 2, 1921, the *Chicago Tribune* announced that the $6,750,000 facility would open the next day.

From its inception in 1857, McVickers theater, located at 25 W. Madison Street, featured high-drama live theater in which women and men performed in a manner consistent with Victorian attitudes toward courtship and romantic love. In the 1920s, in contrast, McVickers became famous for its bawdy vaudeville entertainment. McVickers next became a movie theater, evolving with the times and its preferred forms of entertainment.

The Pastime Theater, located at 66 W. Madison, housed traveling Broadway shows, vaudeville acts, and popular exotica. During the first decades of the century, Chicago established itself as a theater hub, and venues like the Pastime and McVickers, with their elaborate sets and lavish decor, attracted visitors and big-name entertainers to the city.

The Chilton & Thomas dance team, shown here in the late 1920s, were Charleston dancers. New flamboyant and suggestive dances such as the Charleston and the Black Bottom became wildly popular in Chicago's prohibition-era nightclubs. The 1924, all-black musical revue, *Runnin' Wild,* is credited with inspiring the Charleston craze.

Small numbers of women even joined the police ranks in the 1920s. Shown here is Chicago policewoman Anna Sheridan, with pistol, in 1928.

The Pekin Cafe, located on 2700 S. State Street, was the first black-owned and operated vaudeville and theater in Chicago. It was opened by Robert T. Motts in 1905 and served the black community. Many of Chicago's nightlife venues, even those in the black community, remained off-limits to African American patrons, despite the fact that they often featured black entertainers.

The Plantation Cafe, located on 35th Street and Calumet Avenue, was integrated and attracted white patrons as well as black. These clubs, sometimes called black and tans, were some of the only businesses in Chicago with an integrated clientele. Nightclubs like these were often caught up in turf wars as the gangs jockeyed for control of Chicago's nightlife venues and speakeasies. Most of these clubs were either owned by the gangs or they paid protection money to remain open.

Gene Tunney took Jack Dempsey's title after the infamous "long count"—what appeared to many spectators to be an excessively long count by the referee to ensure that Tunney could recover after being knocked down by Dempsey. The fight and the controversy served only to reaffirm Chicago's corrupt reputation.

Prizefighting was illegal in Chicago between 1900 and 1926. Republican Mayor William Hale Thompson legalized the sport during his third term and is shown here with Jack Dempsey in 1927.

William Hale "Big Bill" Thompson was mayor of Chicago from 1915 until 1923 and then again from 1927 until 1931. Thompson was seen, at best, as soft on crime, and at worst, as corrupt. He was criticized for "ethnic baiting," including pandering to black voters, "flip flopping," and general corruption. Under Thompson's administration the gangs thrived.

Charles C. Healey, a former police chief, had been charged with "grafting" after it was discovered he had accepted money from professional gambler Billy Skidmore. Healey was successfully defended by Clarence Darrow and avoided jail time. This event prefigured Darrow's later fame and solidified the questionable reputation of the Chicago Police Department.

"Umbrella" Mike Boyle with his signature accessory. Boyle was a corrupt boss of the electrical workers union who had his bribes dropped into his umbrella. Corruption was so widespread in Chicago that many honest officials were considered crooked.

Corruption in Chicago extended beyond just the realm of politicians, law officers, labor leaders, and sports figures. Shown here, bankers from Wilson Avenue Bank and Mason Bank talk to a reporter and respond to charges of embezzlement.

Harrison B. Riley and Justin M. Dall, president and secretary respectively of Chicago Title and Trust. The two were taken to court for leasing land for "disorderly purposes." Title and Trust was one of the city's oldest leasing companies, having been able to salvage their records from the devastation of the Great Fire of 1871.

Violent crime in Chicago in the 1920s was not limited to gang activity. The criminal courts saw an increase in female defendants, including Beulah Annan and Belva Gaertner, the murderesses featured in the recent musical *Chicago.* Another murderess, Mrs. Rene B. Morrow (pictured here), spent time in the Cook County Jail after her husband's death was ruled a murder rather than a suicide, as first assumed.

The biggest criminal case of the 1920s didn't involve gangsters, sports heroes, or civic leaders. Chicago's "trial of the century" concerned the murder of fourteen-year-old Bobby Franks by elite youths Nathan F. Leopold, Jr., and Richard Loeb. Clarence Darrow's eloquent defense of Leopold and Loeb, in which he argued for rehabilitation over retribution, saved the defendants from the death penalty and captivated the nation by emphasizing the psychological state of the criminals. Darrow, a prominent Chicago attorney who had also defended Eugene Debs and would go on to defend John T. Scopes, was coaxed out of retirement to work on the case.

A crowd outside the office of State's Attorney Robert Crowe. Attorney Crowe, often accused of corruption himself, was the chief prosecutor in the Leopold and Loeb case.

This photograph depicts a group of men near the crime scene where Franks' corpse was hidden. The case received national attention because of the heinous nature of the crime, a thrill killing, and the background of the criminals: both came from prominent Jewish families and were well educated. They also appeared to be involved in a homosexual relationship.

The "perfect crime" was foiled because Nathan Leopold left his eyeglasses at the scene.

James Mulroy and Alvin Goldstein, shown here in 1924, were local reporters who broke the Leopold and Loeb murder case. Chicago's ambitious investigative reporters were seen by some as the only trustworthy voice in the city. They were also frequently accused of embellishing or sensationalizing stories to sell more papers.

The Criminal Court of Cook County at Hubbard and Dearborn streets. It was here that Leopold and Loeb were tried for the murder of young Robert Franks.

The Cook County Jail, where Leopold and Loeb were held during the trial.

Although many gangland criminals spent time behind these walls, in 1924, Chicago's most infamous criminals were two graduate students from the University of Chicago, Nathan F. Leopold, Jr., and Richard Loeb.

William T. Davis, of Cook County jail. Some jailers were intimidated or bribed to allow special privileges for gangsters or wealthy prisoners.

The yard at the Cook County Jail. Leopold and Loeb, like many of Chicago's famous gangsters, were allowed many special privileges, including catered meals and drinking and smoking privileges.

Organized crime was present in Chicago before Capone. In this 1911 photograph, U.S. marshals
Colder and Donovan walk with a handcuffed Gianni Aldoni, who was involved in a Black Hand case.
"Black Hand" refers to a technique of extortion used by gangs in the early twentieth century and was a
precursor to Chicago's more famous and sophisticated gang activity in the 1920s.

Revenge killings were not uncommon before Capone. Here, James Franche crosses the sidewalk with a police officer during the Isaac Henagow murder trial, 1914. Franche confessed to murdering Henagow at the Roy Jones Café on South Wabash Avenue.

James "Big Jim" Colosimo with Attorney Charles Erbstein shortly before Colosimo's murder. Colosimo built his illegal operations around prostitution, running a string of brothels in Chicago. An early prototype of the Chicago gangster, Colosimo maintained good relations with city politicians. Colosimo was likely murdered by Frankie Yale either in an attempt to acquire Colosimo's operations for himself, or under contract for Al Capone and John Torrio.

BIRTH OF THE CHICAGO GANGSTER

(1919–1926)

Violent explosions and gunfire in Chicago were not so common during the gangster era as some might imagine, but they were part of the city's soundtrack. Shown here, a dry goods store at 7303 S. Halsted Street owned by Benjamin Wolfe is destroyed by a bomb. Wolfe maintained that he was the victim of a labor conflict.

A Chicago police officer examines 13 bullet holes in a glass window at the scene of an attempted murder.

Al Capone (left), born on January 17, 1899, in Brooklyn, New York, rose quickly in the organized crime world of Chicago. After moving to the Windy City in 1919 to work under crime boss John Torrio, Capone became second in command after just three years. When Torrio fled Chicago after an attempt on his life in 1925, Capone took over and expanded the criminal operations, reportedly raking in over $100,000,000 a year in illegal dealings. The other man pictured here is likely Isaac Roderick, a bail bondsman.

Capone earned the nickname "Scarface" while working as an eighteen-year-old bouncer in Frankie Yale's Brooklyn bar, the Harvard Inn. Capone's left cheek and neck were cut after he insulted a patron and her brother pulled a knife to defend her honor. Capone always preferred to be photographed on his right side.

This photograph captures Al Capone in court in 1926. He would return in 1929 and then again in 1931, but he was never prosecuted for a Prohibition violation.

Al Capone (seated, center) with associates, including racketeers Jim Emery and Frankie La Porte in Chicago Heights.

A police car sits outside Al Capone's modest home at 7244 Prairie Avenue.

Al's brother, Ralph Capone (left) and Anthony Aresso, two members of Capone's gang. Capone brought many of his family members to Chicago, including his brother Frank, who was killed in a shoot-out with Chicago police on Election Day in Cicero, 1924.

Mrs. Ralph Capone, wife of Al Capone's brother.

Longtime Capone enforcer and bodyguard, "Machine Gun" Jack McGurn, was a key player in Capone's operations. In 1929, he was accused of participating in the St. Valentine's Day massacre.

Frank Nitti (center) was Capone's second in command and ran most of the bootlegging operations carried out by the gang. Nicknamed "the Enforcer," he eventually became boss of Capone's organization when "Scarface" went to jail.

Frankie Yale, a Brooklyn vice lord, was Capone's first boss in organized crime. He likely murdered "Big Jim" Colosimo in Chicago in 1920. In 1928, Capone sent hit men to Brooklyn to kill Yale. One of the tommy guns used in Yale's murder was later linked to the St. Valentine's Day Massacre.

John Scalise and Albert Anselmi (center and right) were infamous hit men who murdered Chicago gangster and Capone rival Dean O'Banion in his flower shop on State Street on November 10, 1924. They murdered Frankie Yale in 1927 and victims of the St. Valentine's Day Massacre in 1929. Scalise was about to be indicted for the massacre when he and Anselmi turned up dead. It is suspected that Capone believed the two were going to turn on him.

Harry Cullett, or "Chicken Harry," a Capone bodyguard, sits on a bench in the Criminal Courts Building on Chicago's Near North Side.

Louis Clementi, a gunman for Capone, and Phillip Mangano of New York's Gambino crime family.

A crew of gangsters lined up in a Chicago jail. From left to right are Mike Bizarro, Joe Aiello, Joe Bubinello, Nick Manzello, and Joe Russio.

A shrewd businessman, Capone streamlined and organized crime operations in Chicago. In addition to establishing suburban headquarters, he ran operations in Chicago out of the Metropole Hotel, 2300 S. Michigan Avenue, the Four Deuces Club at 2222 S. Wabash Avenue (named for its address), and the Lexington Hotel (pictured here) at the corner of Michigan Avenue and 22nd Street.

Capone, Torrio, and the other Chicago gangs were able to do business quite easily under Mayor William Hale "Big Bill" Thompson. But in 1923, Thompson withdrew from the mayoral race and William Dever was elected. Dever ran as a reformer and threatened gang operations in the city. Capone and Torrio decided to move their operations to the sleepy suburb of Cicero, where a weak local government and proximity to Chicago combined to help their organization grow tremendously. In 1927, with the help of Al Capone, Thompson became mayor again.

Eddie Tancl, a former boxer turned saloonkeeper and bootlegger, operated the Hawthorne Cabaret in Cicero until he was shot and killed in 1924, shortly after the Capone-Torrio organization moved in.

Edward "Spike" O'Donnell in 1925. O'Donnell was a South Side gangster embroiled in the Beer Wars of early Prohibition, where rival gangs jockeyed for control over the underground beer trade.

A man points to bullet holes in Edward "Spike" O'Donnell's car. Frank McErlane, O'Donnell's main rival for South Side control, made this unsuccessful attempt on O'Donnell's life in what is reported to be the first gangster crime committed with a Thompson submachine gun, or tommy gun.

Police Chief William Shoemaker points a Thompson submachine gun, or tommy gun, for reporters. Developed for the battlefields of World War I, the tommy gun could fire multiple rounds of ammunition at a very rapid rate, making it popular with gangsters.

Chicago police captain John Stege displays a machine gun concealed inside a violin case.

The Chicago Police Department struggled to curtail the gangs. Widespread corruption on the force and in the judicial system undermined the willingness of many Chicago policemen to put themselves at odds with the powerful and violent Chicago gangs.

Chief of Detectives Captain James Mooney and Chief of Police Colonel John J. Garrity aim handguns for reporters inside a police station. The Chicago police were seen by many as ineffectual at stopping the gangs, and in some cases, as simply corrupt.

Joe Esposito hands out baskets of food to people in 1926. "Diamond Joe" was a politician and gangster serving as Boss of the West Side's 19th Ward. In an operation common to many gangsters and politicians, Esposito was generous both to the people and to the mob men who lived in the communities he controlled. Esposito offered political protection to John Torrio, Capone's mentor.

Originally a friend to John Torrio, Joe Esposito eventually became a rival of Capone. He was shot to death in front of his wife and daughter at the Republican primary on March 21, 1928.

Joe Saltis, partner of Frank McErlane, leaves Chicago's Bridewell police station in 1929. Saltis and politician "Dingbat" O'Berta arranged a conference in the fall of 1926 to call a ceasefire between gangs, including Capone's organization and the North Side Mob run by George Moran. The ceasefire lasted only two months.

Mrs. Joe Saltis, wife of the powerful Southside gangster. Most of the Chicago gang leaders had spouses and many had children.

A crowd gathers for the funeral of John "Dingbat" O'Berta, a politician with considerable ties to Chicago gangs. O'Berta worked closely with Joseph "Polack Joe" Saltis and Frank McErlane during prohibition, even using his political power to get a murder case against himself and Saltis dropped. O'Berta was found dead of a gunshot wound to the head.

Under Mayor Dever's administration, modest headway was made to limit gang activity and curtail bootlegging. In this view, a still is confiscated in a South Side raid.

Captain Willard Malone with rifles, automatic shotguns, machine guns, and ammunition confiscated in raids by police.

Two men pour out barrels of confiscated moonshine. Home-distilled moonshine was fermented in wooden barrels to make it taste more like whiskey.

The gangs made money from all sorts of illegal activity, including prostitution and gambling. Authorities are smashing slot machines in this photograph. As early as 1900, the Chicago Vice Commission's report listed gambling as a main concern.

Illegal pin games confiscated in four tavern raids are examined by Eugene J. Holland, Prosecutor James Jeroulis, and Assistant State's Attorney William Brumlik.

Paraphernalia from another popular crime: counterfeiting. Coin molds are pictured here.

A counterfeit coin–making operation was run out of this building at 6657 S. State Street.

Louis Alterie and Scott Stewart (wearing fedoras, Alterie at left). Alterie was a member of the North Side Gang under mob boss Dean O'Banion and a pallbearer at his funeral. Stewart, a former Chicago DA turned defense attorney, was famous for his creative courtroom antics. He was the inspiration for the fast-talking lawyer Billy Flynn in the musical *Chicago*.

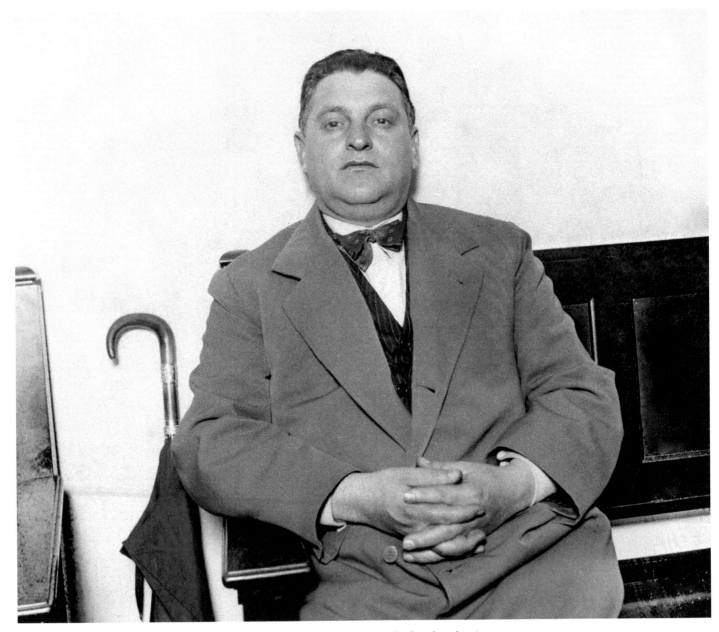

Vincent Genna, known as Jim, was one of the "terrible Gennas," six violent Sicilian bootlegging brothers who operated out of Chicago's Little Italy neighborhood. They had a license to sell "industrial alcohol" and skirted the Prohibition laws easily.

Angelo Genna's funeral. Genna had conspired to have Dean O'Banion killed over bootlegging territory and price disputes. Genna was killed by O'Banion's successors in retaliation. Revenge killing and greed was the cause of most of the inter-gang violence.

Vehicle and guns belonging to the Birger Gang, southern Illinois bootlegging rivals of the Shelton Gang. Testimony from Charles Birger helped put the Shelton brothers in jail and secured the Birger Gang's reign over bootlegging in that region.

The Birger Gang, southern Illinois bootleggers, pose with guns. Charles Birger is at center, on top of the car.

Bootlegger Terry Druggan in court. Druggan's wealth and political clout helped him acquire and maintain multiple breweries in the Chicago area, although he did have to give Capone 40 percent of his profits. Druggan was brought to trial with his partner Frankie Lake. Despite being found guilty, the two bribed the officers in jail and were allowed to come and go as they pleased during their one-year prison term.

One of Terry Druggan's Breweries on 12th Street and Oakley Avenue. In 1924, despite attempts to bribe the courts, Druggan was forced to dump more than 70,000 gallons of illegal alcohol.

"West Side" Frankie Pope being put into an ambulance. Pope ran a gambling spot for Capone in Cicero called the Hawthorne Smoke Shop. Despite many years of what seemed to be loyal service, a dispute over earnings knocked Frankie out of favor with Capone's gang.

Crowd on the street for the funeral of William H. McSwiggin. McSwiggin was a successful assistant prosecutor who had grown up with and remained friends with some of Chicago's infamous gangsters. He was shot on April 27, 1926, by Capone assassins in an attempt to kill the rival gangsters McSwiggin was standing near.

The Lincoln in which McSwiggin was riding the night he was killed. The car was owned by the O'Donnell brothers, rivals of Capone.

The body of Patrick "Paddy" Murray after he was gunned down on State Street October 11, 1926, during the assassination of Earl "Hymie" Weiss. Murray was the personal bodyguard of Weiss, who was shot along with Murray and then died on route to Henrotin Hospital. The month before, Weiss had led an extremely violent attack on Capone's Cicero headquarters in an attempt on his life. He failed. Capone reached out to settle the dispute through an emissary, Tony Lombardo, but when no compromise could be reached, Capone had Weiss killed.

A crowd gathers for the funeral of Hymie Weiss at Sbarbaro's funeral chapel at 708 North Wells Street after the Chicago's Cardinal Mundelein denied Weiss a church service. Weiss was murdered in front of the same flower shop in which Dean O'Banion had been killed two years earlier. After the attack on O'Banion, Weiss and "Bugs" Moran took over the slain gangster's operations.

Weiss was buried October 16, 1926, at Mount Carmel Cemetery in Hillside, Illinois.

Josephine Simard, actress and girlfriend of Hymie Weiss. After his assassination, Simard claimed to be Weiss's spouse and the heir to his estate. The courts eventually awarded the estate to Weiss's mother.

GANGLAND CHICAGO

(1927–1929)

This photograph was taken on election night, April 25, 1927. Republican "Big Bill" Thompson's defeat of reform mayor William Dever was a positive sign to local gang leaders familiar with his chummy relationships with Chicago racketeers.

Jack Zuta, mob accountant for both Al Capone and later Capone's North Side rival George "Bugs" Moran, was responsible for keeping the financial records for the mobsters. These records often listed names of people affiliated with the gangs, including officials on the payroll. After Zuta's murder in 1930, his meticulous records were discovered in various safe deposit boxes, revealing the mob's extensive influence in Chicago's political circles.

Capone bookie Hymie Levine in court (third from left, with dark lapels).

Exterior of Joliet prison, designed by William Boyington, the same architect who designed Chicago's famous Water Tower. At the time it was built in 1858, it was the largest prison in the United States. Many Chicago mobsters spent time inside the fortified walls of this prison.

Bugs Moran's North Side Gang had proved itself to be a stubborn obstacle to Al Capone's total dominance of Chicago bootlegging. Moran was a formidable and ruthless opponent. In this image, a group of investigators examines evidence from a Moran Gang shooting. The man at left holds a tommy gun.

On February 14, 1929, four men, some wearing police uniforms, entered a garage at 2122 N. Clark, owned by gangster George "Bugs" Moran, and murdered seven men. The event became known as the St. Valentine's Day Massacre, and it marked the beginning of the end for Al Capone.

Police and spectators gather in front of the infamous garage. The St. Valentine's Day Massacre became a symbol of the unbridled violence and ruthlessness of Chicago's criminal underworld, especially Al Capone.

Police remove bodies from the scene of the St. Valentine's Day Massacre.

A special crime committee is sworn in over the bodies of the victims of the St. Valentine's Day Massacre. Law enforcement, as well as the public, was outraged by the incident (made even more embarrassing by the use of police uniforms as disguises by the killers), and increased attention was given to Capone's crime syndicate. The result was Eliot Ness's "Untouchable" investigative task force.

Jack McGurn, reputed gangster, and his girlfriend, Louise Rolfe, in court. McGurn was charged with participating in the St. Valentine's Day Massacre, but was acquitted. No one was ever convicted of the murders.

It was widely believed that Capone had ordered the February 14 hit on the Moran Gang.

The 1920s would come to an end before the law caught up to Al Capone.

By 1932, most Democrats and many Republicans opposed Prohibition. This photograph depicts the Republican Citizens Committee campaigning for the repeal of the 18th Amendment that year. Arguments for the repeal included that prohibition hurt the economy and that it stimulated criminal activity. The 18th Amendment was repealed by President Franklin Delano Roosevelt in 1933.

The End of the Capone Era

(1930–1939)

Unemployed Chicagoans numbering 2,000 to 3,000 gather at Monroe and Sangamon streets on February 29, 1932, to protest worsening economic and living conditions. The Great Depression hit Chicago's economy especially hard.

While the city cracked down on Capone's illegal activities, Capone was busy rebuilding his reputation. Capone opened his own soup kitchen in Chicago. He saw in the privations of the Great Depression an opportunity to improve his public image.

Al Capone at a baseball game at Comiskey Park, 1931. Before the end of the baseball season, Capone would be indicted on charges of tax evasion and failure to file tax returns.

Capone's tax evasion trial was the event of the day and drew large crowds outside the Federal Building in Chicago hoping to catch a glimpse of the well-known gangster.

Capone with attorneys Mike Ahern and Albert Fink at his 1931 trial.

Capone, shown here with his attorney Mike Ahern, was charged with failure to pay taxes on his illegal earnings. Capone initially pled guilty thinking he could negotiate a plea agreement. But Judge James H. Wilkerson made it clear that there would be no deals for Capone.

Capone was sentenced to a total of 11 years in prison, 10 years in a federal penitentiary and 1 year in the county jail. Capone was stunned by the severity of the sentence as were his lawyers and most of the reporters covering the case.

Capone's jury on a lunch break during the trial. Capone's plan to manipulate the jurors was thwarted when Judge Wilkerson swapped Capone's jury for another one impaneled to hear a different case. On October 25, 1931, the untainted twelve found Capone guilty.

The police bus outside the Cook County Jail, where Capone would spend his first night after being sentenced by Judge Wilkerson.

Capone was first sent to the federal penitentiary in Atlanta to begin serving his sentence. It was quickly discovered that he was obtaining special privileges and exerting influence on the prison population. He was then moved to Alcatraz to finish his term. This move effectively cut Capone off from his powerbase. He could only serve his time and hope that he would still have influence upon his release.

While in prison Capone's syphilitic dementia forced him into the prison hospital for the remainder of his incarceration.

The Morrison Hotel, at Madison and Clark streets, served as the unofficial headquarters of Mayor Anton Cermak. Shortly after Cermak was sworn in he tightened the political clampdown on organized crime. On February 15, 1933, Cermak was shot while shaking hands with Franklin Delano Roosevelt in Florida. He died March 6 from his wounds.

Cermak was only the second Chicago mayor to be assassinated and his funeral was well attended. Cermak was the father of Chicago's Democratic machine, and he and his successor, Edward Kelly, were strongly supported by FDR.

The repeal of Prohibition inspired celebration. Chicago's underworld, however, would find ways other than bootlegging to remain a potent force in the city into the 1930s and throughout the remainder of the century.

This photograph of Legionnaires celebrating was taken at the repeal of the 18th Amendment in 1933.

Violent attacks, such as this tavern bombing at 1206 W. Madison Street in September 1937, reminded Chicagoans that the gangs hadn't left town with Capone.

In 1934, the Dells Roadhouse in Morton Grove, a suburb of Chicago, was torched by three men with submachine guns after they kidnapped and blindfolded the caretaker.

Capone's influence quickly waned, but the gangs persevered and the violence continued, eventually touching some of Capone's former cohorts. In this photograph, Chicago police search Jack McGurn's automobile for fingerprints after his murder in a bowling alley at 805 Milwaukee Avenue.

A hearse takes "Machine Gun" Jack McGurn to his final resting place.

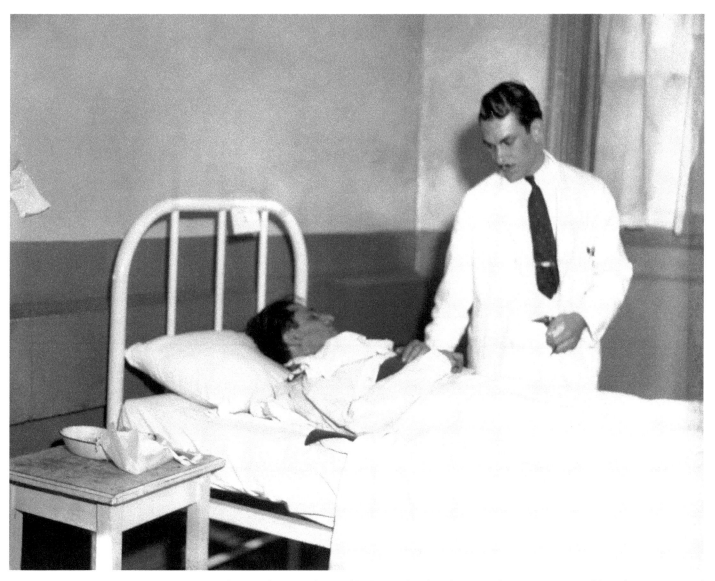

Frank Nitti, here in a hospital bed, was shot by Chicago policemen in 1932. Although Nitti survived the ordeal and managed to regain power over his organization, he was eventually indicted for extortion, along with many other gangsters, in 1943. Nitti never showed up for his day in court. Instead, he shot himself in the head the morning of his grand jury appearance.

The growth of national crime-fighting forces, aimed at destroying the well-organized urban gangs of the 1920s, resulted in high-profile arrests and convictions across the nation. The FBI manhunt to capture bank robber and escaped convict John Dillinger (pictured here in court) ended in an alley behind Chicago's Biograph Theater at 2433-43 N. Lincoln Avenue on July 22, 1934.

Capone was released from prison in 1939. He moved to his home in Palm Island, Florida, mentally unfit to run his criminal organization, and died of pneumonia on January 25, 1947. His body was brought back to Chicago and buried in Mount Olivet Cemetery near the graves of his father and brother. He was later moved to Mount Carmel Cemetery on Chicago's West Side.

"A Map of Chicago's gangland from authentic sources: designed to inculcate the most important principles of piety and virtue in young persons, and graphically portray the evils and sin of large cities." Issued in 1931 by cartographers Bruce-Roberts Inc., the map identifies key gang territories in the city from which the gangs controlled the distribution and sale of liquor during Prohibition.

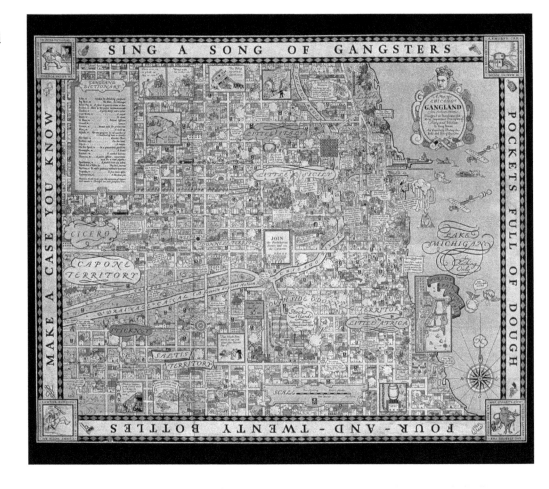

Chicago at the end of the Capone era.

NOTES ON THE PHOTOGRAPHS

These notes, listed by page number, attempt to include all aspects known of the photographs. Each of the photographs is identified by the page number, a title or description, photographer and collection, archive, and call or box number when applicable. Although every attempt was made to collect all data, in some cases complete data may have been unavailable due to the age and condition of some of the photographs and records.

II   ST. VALENTINE'S DAY
      MASSACRE
      Chicago History Museum
      DN-0087709

VI   CAPTAIN GOLDBERG
      Chicago History Museum
      ICHi-03611

X   NORTH LAKE SHORE
      DRIVE
      Chicago History Museum
      ICHi-19436

2   ARMISTICE DAY
      Chicago History Museum
      DN-0070558

3   WOMEN'S SUFFRAGE
      CROWD W/ SPEAKER
      Chicago History Museum
      DN-0066345

4   JUVENILE COURT
      BUILDING AND
      DETENTION HOME
      Chicago History Museum
      ICHi-51228

5   SALOON
      Chicago History Museum
      DN-0003965

6   PROHIBITION
      Chicago History Museum
      ICHi-03613

7   RACE RIOTS, OGDEN
      CAFE
      Chicago History Museum
      ICHi-29663

8   INVESTIGATING
      BEATING
      Chicago History Museum
      ICHi-30857

9   WHITE SOX PLAYERS
      Chicago History Museum
      ICHi-32253

10   JUDGE LANDIS IN
      COURTROOM
      Chicago History Museum
      DN-0062284

11   CROWD WATCHING
      PLANES
      Chicago History Museum
      DN-0092747

12   DRAKE HOTEL 1926
      Chicago History Museum
      ICHi-00708

13   FIELD MUSEUM
      Chicago History Museum
      ICHi-51232

14   MCVICKERS THEATER
      Chicago History Museum
      ICHi-51234

15   THE PASTIME THEATER
      Chicago History Museum
      DN-0068755

16   CHILTON & THOMAS
      DANCE TEAM MEMBERS
      Chicago History Museum
      ICHi-16225

17   CHICAGO
      POLICEWOMAN ANNA
      SHERIDAN
      Chicago History Museum
      DN-0084697

18   THE PEKIN CAFE
      Chicago History Museum
      ICHi-20428

19   THE PLANTATION CAFE
      Chicago History Museum
      ICHi-14428

20   GENE TUNNEY TAKING
      THE TITLE
      Chicago History Museum
      SDN-066970a

21   PRIZEFIGHTING
      Chicago History Museum
      ICHi-26572

22   BIG BILL
      Chicago History Museum
      DN-0064828

23   CHARLES C. HEALEY
      Chicago History Museum
      DN-0067144

24   "UMBRELLA" MIKE
      BOYLE
      Chicago History Museum
      DN-0067691

25   ON THE SIDEWALK
      Chicago History Museum
      ICHi-51239

26   HARRISON B. RILEY
      AND JUSTIN M. DALL
      Chicago History Museum
      ICHi-51240

27   EXITING THE JAIL
      Chicago History Museum
      ICHi-51236

28   DARROW DEFENDING
      LEOPOLD AND LOEB
      Chicago History Museum
      DN-0077498

29   CROWD
      Chicago History Museum
      ICHi-51241

30   CRIME SCENE
      Chicago History Museum
      DN-0077253

Printed in the USA
CPSIA information can be obtained
at www.ICGtesting.com
JSHW072023140824
68134JS00042B/3763